BELIEVE IT!

A Texas Rangers World Championship 63 Years in the Making

Book design by **Josh Crutchmer**

Photos courtesy of **AP Images** and **Getty Images**

ISBN: 9978-1-957005-20-1

Printed in the United States of America

CONTENTS

On Top of the World

THE TEXAS RANGERS — World Champions!

Sounds pretty good, doesn't it? Texas fans have waited 63 long years to utter those words, and finally, the Rangers are on top.

Let the celebration begin!

Having lost 102 games just two years ago, the Rangers completed their incredible turnaround by beating a talented Arizona Diamondbacks team 5-0 to win the World Series 4-1.

In the following pages we proudly take you on a trip down memory lane of this championship season that came to its jubilant conclusion Phoenix, AZ.

Believe It! provides Rangers fans the best view in the house of all the ups and downs of the season and gives you an inside look at the incredible World Series win 63 years in the making.

Our heartfelt congratulations go out to Texas GM Chris Young, Manager Bruce Bochy and his staff, and the entire Rangers team on their accomplishments this season.

Celebrate this season and save this book to revisit the Rangers' magical moments and unforgettable team – both stars and role players – who rewarded your faith with a World Championship.

Congratulations Texas Rangers!

The Rangers celebrate after winning the 2023 World Series in five games over the Arizona Diamondbacks.

Battery Powered

Rangers Rally at the Plate for Wild Day One Win Over Phillies

ARLINGTON, Texas —

JACOB DEGROM AND AARON NOLA didn't have the kind of pitchers' duel that many had anticipated when they faced off in the season opener.

Robbie Grossman and Brad Miller homered in a big comeback for Texas after prized acquisition deGrom struggled in his debut, and the Rangers beat Nola and the National League champion Philadelphia Phillies 11-7 on Thursday.

"I'm just glad I don't have to face (deGrom) anymore," said Grossman, adding that the pitcher will pick up the team plenty this season. "All I can say is baseball is back and the rollercoaster of emotions in the season."

Grossman, a free-agent addition who earned the starting left field job in spring training, hit a three-run homer that tied the game at 5-5 in the middle of a nine-run outburst in the fourth inning. An inning later, Miller became the first Rangers player in 11 years to homer in consecutive season openers. His two-run shot made it 11-6.

While deGrom struck out seven without a walk, the two-time National League Cy Young Award winner allowed five runs on six extra-base hits in his 3 2/3 innings. He threw 49 of 73 pitches for strikes. DeGrom signed a $185 million, five-year contract in free agency and made his fourth career start on opening day — he threw 17 scoreless innings in his three openers for the New York Mets, his team the last nine seasons.

Nola, the 29-year-old right-hander making his sixth and maybe final opening-day start for the Phillies, also allowed five runs on four hits in 3 2/3 innings — he didn't allow a hit the first three. Nola is in the final year of his contract and discussions about an extension ended just before the start of the season.

"The first inning took its toll on him, because it was a long inning, 21, 22 pitches," Phillies manager Rob Thomson said. "Then got the ball up for the last inning, probably missed some locations."

The game also marked the Rangers debut of Bruce Bochy, the three-time World Series champion who was back in the dugout after a three-year retirement for his 26th opener as a manager. He had previously managed 13 seasons with the San Francisco Giants, who clinched their 2010 title in Texas, and 12 seasons with the San Diego Padres.

"After a tough start, a great way to finish it," Bochy said of the nine-run fourth that matched the highest-scoring inning ever in a season opener for Texas.

The Phillies took a 5-0 lead when No. 9 hitter Brandon Marsh, the first batter after deGrom departed, had an RBI double off Cole Ragans (1-0).

....

Rangers relief pitcher Jonathan Hernandez begins his windup as the newly instituted pitch clock winds down.

Phillies first baseman Darick Hall reaches out to tag Rangers' Nathaniel Lowe during the fourth inning of the season opener.

The Phillies and Rangers stand for the national anthem at Globe Life Field on Opening Day.

Familiar Faces Abound

A Year Before Hosting, Rangers Load Up AL All-Star Roster

SEATTLE —

IN THE SECOND INNING OF TUESDAY NIGHT'S MLB All-Star Game, American League starting catcher Jonah Heim looked out from behind home plate and recognized more than a few familiar faces.

The Rangers had four position players join Heim in the AL's starting lineup, including Marcus Semien, Corey Seager, Adolis García and Josh Jung. When pitcher Nathan Eovaldi took the mound in the second inning, Texas made history by becoming the first club to have six players on the field at the same time in an All-Star Game since the 1951 Brooklyn Dodgers.

A ball thrown by Eovaldi during that inning and signed by the Rangers on the field is on its way to the National Baseball Hall of Fame in Cooperstown, NY.

"That's gotta be one of the cooler moments in sports when you got half the team on the field is your own team and in an All-Star Game," Heim said before the NL rallied for a 3-2 victory. "I was glad I got to share the deal with these guys today."

"It's incredible," Eovaldi added. "I've been fortunate. Obviously, we overlook these little things during the season, because we get to be around each other all the time. But to be able to share this moment with those guys, everything that we put in, it means the world, it's awesome."

It's fitting that the Rangers would overload this year's All-Star squad, considering they hope to do the same in their home ballpark in 2024. The club will host the Midsummer Classic at Globe Life Field next year in what will be the ballpark's fifth season.

"You heard the fans when they announced all the Seattle players," Heim said. "So I think if that happens, and we got five starters, again, it's gonna be really loud in Globe Life. It's gonna be a cool environment and it's gonna be a blast."

The Rangers' players are just as excited as everybody else to be able to host the event in their home stadium, especially coming off the star-studded 2023 in Seattle.

A native of Alvin, Texas, Eovaldi knows how exciting it'll be for the entire state and region to be able to showcase itself to the entire baseball world. And hopefully even more Rangers can take the field.

"We're excited," Eovaldi said. "I think it's gonna be great up in Arlington, especially for the state of Texas. We've got a new stadium so everybody's gonna get to experience that, especially for our fans. We've been able to have a lot of fans showing support and things like that, so I think it'll be really fun."

Adolis García of the Rangers catches a fly ball hit by Sean Murphy of the Braves during the All-Star Game.

Marcus Semien (left) and Josh Jung of the Rangers stand in the dugout with Austin Hays of the Orioles before the All-Star Game.

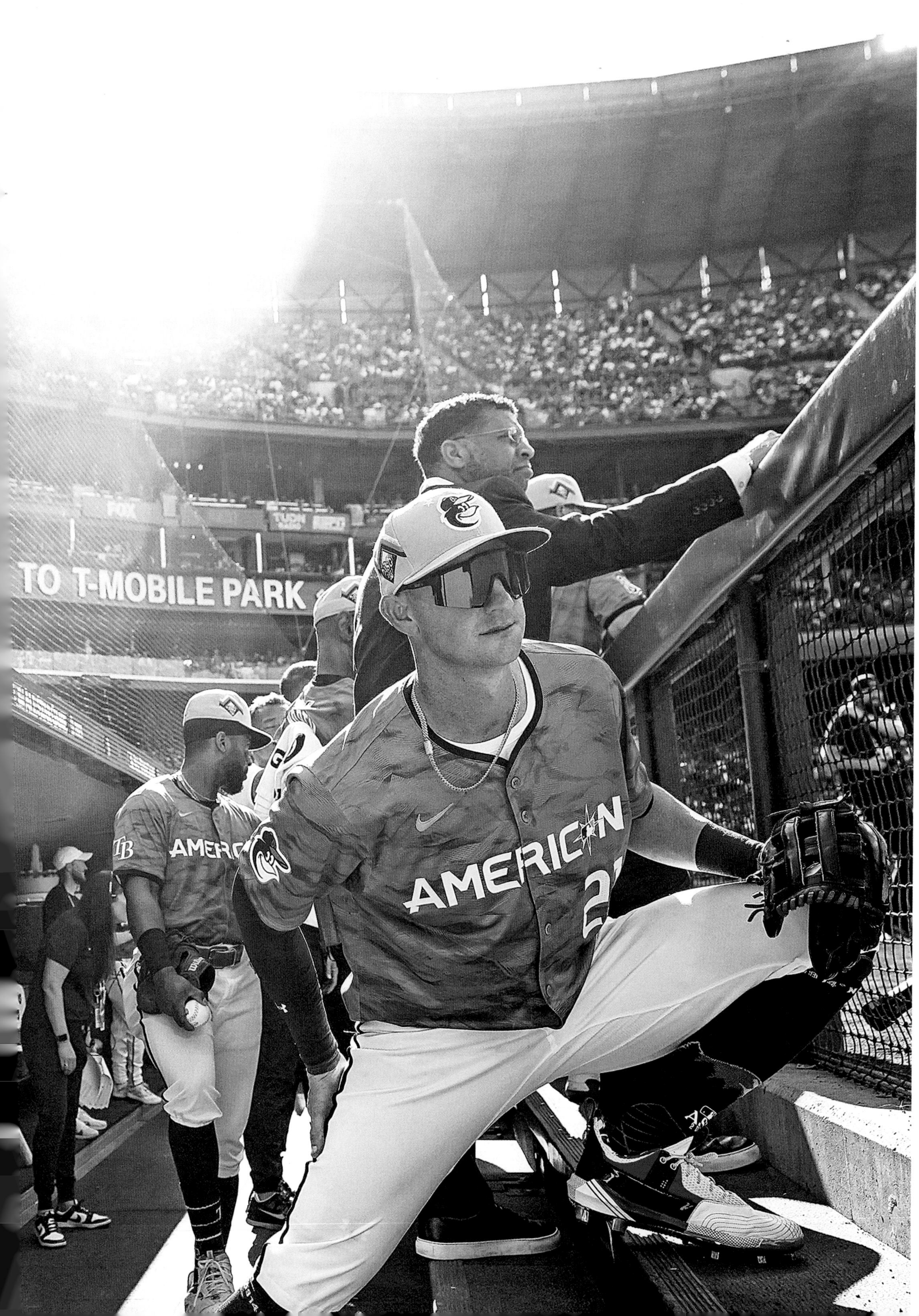
TO T-MOBILE PARK
AMERICAN
AMERICAN
FOX

Six in a Row!

Speas Sparkles, Heim Homers, Rangers Roll

ARLINGTON, Texas —

ALEX SPEAS STRUCK OUT his first three batters in his big league debut for the Texas Rangers, getting two outs with his first one when All-Star catcher Jonah Heim threw out a runner trying to steal second base.

That relief from Speas, a second-round draft pick in 2016, came before Heim's big three-run homer in the eighth inning as the AL West leaders stretched their winning streak to six games with a 5-1 victory over the slumping Tampa Bay Rays on Wednesday.

The Rays (60-39) are 3-11 in July, and not alone atop the AL East for the first time since being tied after winning on opening day as part of their 13-0 start. Baltimore (58-37) is ahead by percentage points after an 8-5 win over the Los Angeles Dodgers.

Texas manager Bruce Bochy was looking for a soft landing spot for the debut of the 25-year-old Speas, who last year was coaching youth baseball. It didn't quite work out that way, but the reliever looked quite comfortable anyway.

Speas had been through Tommy John surgery, the birth of his daughter and the COVID-19-shortened 2020 season without any games to play before stepping away from the pros.

"Being honest, fighting mental health sometimes is not the easiest thing to do. There's some long nights, there's some long days, and it's a hard fight to get through it all," he said. "But glad we made it here. And I thank the organization for having trust in me and giving me the opportunity to come back and do this."

The Rays, who host Baltimore in a four-game series starting Thursday, had 10 hits. But they got their only run on Jose Siri's 19th homer with one out in the ninth.

"We just couldn't get anything going, and that's the way it goes sometimes, but it does feel like it is accumulating quite a bit," Rays manager Kevin Cash said.

Texas (58-39) wrapped up its second three-game series sweep since the All-Star break, and it has its longest win streak since also winning six in a row in 2019. Leody Taveras hit his 11th homer on the first pitch of the third against Zack Littell (0-2), and he added an RBI single in the seventh.

Brock Burke (4-2) struck out three over two scoreless innings in relief of starter Jon Gray.

Speas took over with one out in the seventh, which ended with pinch-hitter Wander Franco striking out on the same pitch that Manuel Margot was thrown out trying to steal. Speas then pitched a perfect eighth with two more strikeouts — of leadoff hitter Yandy Díaz, who dropped to the ground after one of the fastballs, and Randy Arozarena.

"I can't say enough about what he did. That kid really showed great poise, really handled the situation so well," Bochy said.

....

Rangers relief pitcher Alex Speas throws his first pitch as he makes his Major-League debut against the Rays.

Rangers catcher Jonah Heim tags out the Rays' Josh Lowe at home plate.

A Turning Point

Benches Clear but Rangers Blow Out Defending Champions

HOUSTON —

ADOLIS GARCÍA HIT A GRAND SLAM to highlight a seven-run fifth inning and the AL West-leading Texas Rangers slugged four homers in a 13-5 win over the Houston Astros in a tense game Wednesday night.

Following his grand slam, García and Marcus Semien exchanged words with Martín Maldonado. That led to the benches and bullpens emptying. No punches were thrown in the scrum around home plate, but Maldonado and Semien were ejected.

"After I scored on Adolis' grand slam, I told (Maldonado), 'I told you we were going to win this game,' and all of sudden, their bench is out there and both of us are out of the game," Semien said. "I didn't want to get thrown out of the game. I just was talking to him."

Maldonado said he was told he was ejected for starting the benches clearing situation.

"Two guys competing against each other and exchanging words," Maldonado said of what led to the benches clearing. "Two teams that want to win. It's something that happens between the lines."

Tempers were hot earlier in the game. Both benches were warned in the third inning after Houston's Framber Valdez hit Semien in the left shoulder with the first pitch of his at-bat. The Rangers' Andrew Heaney had hit Yordan Alvarez in the right shoulder with a pitch in the first inning.

"Obviously, Andrew did not try to hit Yordan, and I got hit with a four-seam fastball from a sinkerballer," Semien said. "I felt like it was on purpose. I walked to first base. I ended up scoring on the home run, and I told Martín, 'We're going to win this game.' We proceeded to score 11 runs after that. I said 'I told you,' and I ended up out of the game."

Semien, Nathaniel Lowe and Sam Huff also homered for Texas, which avoided a three-game sweep and held on to its two-game lead over the Astros in the division.

"Not just to win today, but how we won," Texas manager Bruce Bochy said. "To get down, how we responded after Marcus got drilled. You're talking about karma at its finest, I really think that was the case because there's no way Andrew's trying to hit somebody. He's ahead in the count, and we're trying to get him out of the first inning."

Lowe hit a two-run homer in the third.

Texas got to Valdez (8-7) for four more runs in the fourth. Leody Taveras had a two-run single and Semien hit a two-run homer. Maldonado appeared to exchange words with Semien, who held his finger to his mouth, following the home run.

Huff hit a solo home run to begin the fifth.

Semien had three hits, and Lowe and Taveras each had two hits and three RBI.

Rangers players cool down after the benches cleared during a 13-5 win at Houston on July 26.

Texas' Adolis García, right, celebrates with third base coach Tony Beasley after hitting a grand slam during the fifth inning.

Playoff Bound!

Rangers Headed to Postseason for First Time Since 2016

SEATTLE —

BRUCE BOCHY HAD A BOTTLE OF BUBBLY in his hand as he watched the celebration of a turnaround that very few expected in his first season in charge in Texas.

"This is what I came back for and there's nothing like it," Bochy said. "It's been some kind of ride so far and we've got a lot of work to do but to be in this moment right now these are memories you never forget and for these guys I couldn't be happier."

The Rangers are back in the postseason for the first time since 2016, beating the Seattle Mariners 6-1 on Saturday to clinch a playoff spot in the American League.

Texas (90-71) can claim the AL West title and the No. 2 seed in the AL playoffs with a win over the Mariners in the regular-season finale or a loss by Houston (89-72) at Arizona on Sunday.

After a traditional clinching celebration in the middle of the clubhouse, the Rangers crowded into a dining room to watch the final outs of Houston's 1-0 win over the Diamondbacks. That win pushed the division race to the final day and muted a little of the party.

But just a little.

"To come from where we did last year to make the playoffs is extremely exciting. That's why we're celebrating tonight," Texas shortstop Corey Seager said.

The win by the Astros also eliminated the Mariners from the postseason race, falling short a year after ending a 21-year playoff drought.

It led to some frustration in Seattle's clubhouse, especially after the Mariners made minimal moves at the trade deadline while other contenders, including Texas, were far more aggressive.

"We got to commit to winning," Seattle catcher Cal Raleigh said. "We have to commit to going and getting those players you see other teams going out, going for, getting big-time pitchers, getting big-time hitters and we have to do that to keep up."

The Rangers grabbed control by putting together a four-run third inning against Luis Castillo, highlighted by two-out hits from Nathaniel Lowe, Jonah Heim and Leody Tavares that all plated runs. Heim hit a two-run single with an 0-2 count after fouling off three straight pitches, and Tavares' broken-bat RBI single made it 4-0.

That was all Andrew Heaney and three relievers needed in shutting down the Mariners. Heaney learned late Friday night he would get the call after Jon Gray went on the 15-day injured list with a forearm strain.

It was his first start since Sept. 4 and he worked into the fifth inning before turning it over to the Texas bullpen.

"I was hoping it would be me. They put a lot of faith in me. I really appreciate that," Heaney

Rangers manager Bruce Bochy hugs first baseman Nathaniel Lowe after clinching a playoff berth.

said. "It's been a Jekyll and Hyde (season). I've had some really great ones, some really bad ones. For them to put the faith in me that's amazing."

It's the ninth postseason appearance for the Rangers, but after reaching the playoffs five times between 2010-16, it's been a rough stretch for Texas.

The turnaround with Bochy as manager was dramatic. Texas reached 90 wins for the ninth time in franchise history, and the Rangers already have made a 22-game improvement over last season when they finished with 68 wins.

The Rangers were on the verge of clinching a playoff spot on Thursday night, only to see Seattle rally with two runs in the ninth inning for a 3-2 victory. They were shut out 8-0 on Friday.

But Texas made Castillo work from the outset, eliminating any momentum that might have carried over from the prior two nights.

Bochy is the 12th manager to take three different teams to the postseason after previously going to the playoffs with San Francisco and San Diego.

"We're still trying to win this division. But to get there you work too hard from spring training to pass this up. You got to enjoy it. You got to celebrate," Bochy said.

Castillo (14-9) was pulled after 2 2/3 innings, the shortest start in his 1½ seasons with the Mariners and tied for the second-shortest start of his career. The right-hander had pitched at least five innings in his previous 32 starts this season but nibbled too much on the edges and

Nathaniel Lowe follows through on an RBI single against the Mariners.

found himself in trouble.

Castillo needed 86 pitches to record eight outs. He went to 3-2 counts to seven of the 18 batters he faced and his five walks were one off his season high.

In his final two starts of the regular season, Castillo allowed nine earned runs in 8 2/3 innings.

"It wasn't vintage Luis Castillo today," Seattle manager Scott Servais said. "He was just off a little bit today and they took advantage of it."

Seattle also had some trouble at the plate.

The Mariners loaded the bases in the fifth on singles by Ty France, Sam Haggerty and J.P. Crawford. Heaney was lifted and Josh Sborz (6-7) got Texas out of the jam by retiring Julio Rodríguez and Eugenio Suárez.

Nathaniel Lowe jumps up to celebrate with Josh Jung after beating Seattle 6-1.

The Rangers celebrate on the field after clinching their first playoff spot since 2016.

An Easy Opening

Montgomery Sparkles as Rangers Rout Hapless Rays

ST. PETERSBURG, Fla. —

JORDAN MONTGOMERY WAS EXCEPTIONAL against the Tampa Bay Rays, even better when he lumbered off the mound to make a diving catch that helped the Texas Rangers to a 4-0 victory in their AL Wild Card Series opener.

"It's good to do your job and help the team win," Montgomery said after scattering six hits over seven innings to move the Rangers within a victory of an AL Division Series matchup against the Baltimore Orioles.

Texas rebounded from a weekend collapse that cost the Rangers the AL West title and a first-round playoff bye. The Rays dropped a club-record sixth straight postseason game dating to Game 2 of the 2021 AL Division Series against Boston.

Montgomery's pitching set the tone as the best-of-three series began. The Rangers also drew inspiration from the 6-foot-6 left-hander's defensive gem on a bunt that Jose Siri popped into the air along the first-base line with runners at the corners.

Montgomery dove to make the catch and landed awkwardly.

"I saw it high enough in the air, kind of made two quick steps at it, and then just blacked out and went for it," Montgomery said.

"That was electric. I was fired up," said rookie left fielder Evan Carter, who doubled twice and drew a pair of walks in his postseason debut.

"It wasn't a soft landing was it? He's a big fellow," Rangers manager Bruce Bochy said. "Great catch by him. We were in a tight situation there. ... Just shows you how competitive he is to go out there and dive for that ball."

Bochy and Rangers athletic trainers went to the mound to check on Montgomery, who was not injured.

"I think I was just as shocked as everybody in the stands. I had to backhand it. ... It just was something I've never done before," the pitcher said. "I don't know if I've done that since I was 12. Just kind of a heat-of-the-moment competitive thing."

Corey Seager and Josh Jung drove in runs and the Rangers benefitted from four errors by the Rays, who also fizzled offensively before a crowd of just 19,704 — roughly 5,300 below listed capacity — at Tropicana Field.

"We didn't hit, pitch or defend," Rays manager Kevin Cash said. "When you're up against a good team, they're going to capitalize, and they eventually really did."

Rangers pitcher Jordan Montgomery delivers against the Rays in the first game of the AL Wild-Card series.

Evan Carter, right, hits a double in the fourth inning as Tampa Bay catcher Rene Pinto looks on.

Bounceback Complete

After Rough End to Regular Season, Rangers Enjoy Sweep

ST. PETERSBURG, Fla. —

TWO YEARS AFTER LOSING 102 GAMES, the resilient Texas Rangers are savoring a journey that's transformed them into a playoff team.

"It's all about bouncing back, dealing with the tough times. You know you're going to have them," manager Bruce Bochy said after the Rangers beat the Tampa Bay Rays 7-1 to finish a two-game AL Wild Card Series sweep.

"What's important is how you handle it, and these guys have handled it so well," Bochy added. "I think we were counted out earlier in the season or late August ... but what a job they did to bounce back and to be in this position."

The Rangers rode a rollercoaster of emotions while losing three of four games at Seattle and letting the AL West division title slip away on the final day of the regular season. Instead of returning home with a first-round playoff bye, Texas was rewarded with a cross-country flight to Florida.

"We had to fly right over Dallas, so that could have been really a downer for the club," said Bochy, a first-year manager with Texas after winning three titles with San Francisco. "They reset, refocused, and just put together two of the best games back-to-back that we probably have had all year when you look at the pitching, the offense, the defense — everything we knew we had to do to beat a club like Tampa."

Adolis García and Evan Carter, a 20-year-old rookie who became the second-youngest postseason player in franchise history, homered off Zach Eflin, a 16-game winner unable to save Tampa Bay's season.

Nathan Eovaldi gave Texas an outstanding pitching performance. The Rays' scoreless streak reached 33 innings, one shy of the postseason record held by the 1966-74 Los Angeles Dodgers, before Curtis Mead's RBI single in the seventh.

Texas won a postseason series for the first time since 2011, when the Rangers reached the World Series before losing to St. Louis.

Meanwhile, Tampa Bay followed a stellar start with a fizzling finish.

The Rays opened 13-0 to match the 1982 Atlanta Braves and 1987 Milwaukee Brewers, trailing only the 20-0 start by the 1884 St. Louis Maroons of the Union Association. They led the AL East from opening day and then were overtaken by the Orioles in mid-July.

After gaining the AL's top wild card, Tampa Bay extended its postseason losing streak to seven straight.

Rays manager Kevin Cash didn't offer any excuses for being swept again.

Adolis García gestures after hitting a solo home run against the Rays in the fourth inning of Game 2.

"Look, that's the easy narrative," Cash said. "We are who we are, and we finished the regular season with the guys that we had. I still feel that we could have had a better showing with the roster that we had."

Eovaldi, beating the Rays for the third time this year, allowed six hits while striking out eight and walking none over 6 2/3 innings.

García's leadoff homer began a four-run fourth inning against Eflin. Josh Jung had an RBI triple and Carter hit a two-run homer to right for the Rangers, 7-0 in postseason games at Tropicana Field.

Carter batted .306 with five homers and 12 RBI over 23 games after making his major league debut on Sept. 8. He reached base in his first six postseason at-bats, doubling twice and drawing three walks.

Tampa Bay finally got an out from the No. 9 hole when Colin Poche fanned Carter in the sixth inning. Marcus Semien and Corey Seager followed with run-scoring doubles.

"Carter, gosh, this young kid has come up — I don't even know if he knows that he's in the big leagues," Bochy said. "This guy has such a calmness about him."

Josh Jung congratulates Evan Carter after Carter hit a home run that scored Jung.

Rangers shortstop Corey Seager throws to first after putting out Curtis Mead at second to turn a double play in the fifth inning.

Texas players celebrate after beating Tampa Bay 7-1 to sweep the wild-card matchup.

Shaky, but Unscathed

Rangers' Bullpen Struggles but Holds off Baltimore Bats

BALTIMORE —

FOR THE FIRST TIME THIS POSTSEASON, the maligned Texas bullpen had to protect a slim lead in the late innings.

Josh Sborz, Aroldis Chapman and José Leclerc wobbled but didn't fall.

Andrew Heaney and Dane Dunning helped Texas reach the sixth inning ahead, and the Rangers held on through some anxious moments for a 3-2 victory over the Baltimore Orioles in Game 1 of their AL Division Series.

"The bullpen did a great job," manager Bruce Bochy said. "Got bumpy, but found a way to get through it."

Josh Jung homered and made a nice play at third base to start a critical double play for Texas, which improved to 3-0 in these playoffs — all on the road.

After leading the AL West most of the season but squandering the division crown on the final weekend, the wild-card Rangers entered the postseason without Jacob deGrom and Max Scherzer — and with a bullpen largely considered a weak link. But they've allowed only three runs in three games against the Orioles and Rays.

The late innings weren't all that stressful in the Wild Card Series against Tampa Bay, as Texas outscored the Rays 11-1 for a two-game sweep. It was a more nervous finish against the Orioles.

Heaney held Baltimore to a run and two hits in 3 2/3 innings. Dunning relieved him and went two innings for the win, allowing a run in the sixth. Will Smith, Sborz, Chapman and Leclerc combined for the final 10 outs — but not without some drama.

Sborz threw seven straight balls to start the seventh but pitched around a leadoff walk. Chapman walked the first two batters in the eighth before Jung ranged to his left and snagged Anthony Santander's high bouncer on a short hop to start a 5-4-3 double play. Chapman then struck out Ryan Mountcastle with a runner on third to end the inning.

Leclerc earned the save, although he allowed a leadoff single in the ninth to Gunnar Henderson. All-Star catcher Jonah Heim threw out Henderson trying to steal second, and the Orioles didn't manage another baserunner.

Baltimore manager Brandon Hyde didn't appear happy in the dugout with Henderson's decision to go.

"A little miscommunication there," Hyde said.

Kyle Bradish struck out nine in 4 2/3 innings for the Orioles but allowed two runs in the fourth to take the loss.

Jung and Santander traded solo homers in the sixth.

....

Rangers relief pitcher José Leclerc is congratulated by catcher Jonah Heim at the end of Game 1 of the ALDS.

Josh Jung hits a solo home run in the sixth inning against Baltimore.

Magic Touch is Back

Bochy Finds Another Postseason Groove, Rangers Cruise

BALTIMORE —

BRUCE BOCHY IS ROLLING THROUGH ANOTHER POSTSEASON where everything he tries seems to work.

Mitch Garver hit a third-inning grand slam in his first appearance of these playoffs, and the Texas Rangers won their fourth consecutive game to start the postseason, pushing the Baltimore Orioles to the brink of elimination with an 11-8 victory in Game 2 of the AL Division Series.

The wild-card Rangers have outscored the Orioles and Tampa Bay — the top two teams in the American League in the regular season — by 25-11. Bochy moved within one win of his first AL Championship Series as a manager. He reached that round four times in the National League, winning three World Series titles with San Francisco.

"It's kind of hard to read the emotion on him because sometimes he looks like he's folded up in a lawn chair sitting there watching the game," Garver said. "But yes, we trust his decisions and the way he manages the game."

Gunnar Henderson and Aaron Hicks homered for the AL East champion Orioles, who haven't been swept in a series of at least two games since May 2022. They're now in danger of doing that at a most inopportune time.

Hicks drove in five runs, including a three-run shot with one out in the ninth. But it was too little, too late.

Texas fell behind for the first time this postseason when the Orioles scored two runs in the first, but the Rangers answered with five in the second to knock out rookie Grayson Rodriguez. Garver, a backup catcher who hadn't played yet in the 2023 playoffs, hit his grand slam for a 9-2 lead.

"He can hit, and he's done a great job this year for us," Bochy said. "So gave him the start today. Got a pitch he could handle. He's got big power, and that's big at that point in the game. Really was the difference in the game."

Garver came up again with the bases loaded in the fifth but hit into a double play. Even that brought home another run.

Garver was in the lineup as the designated hitter because it was "just time to get him out there" — to quote Bochy pregame. He hit .270 with 19 home runs in 87 games this year.

There were plenty of other contributors for the Rangers.

Corey Seager became the first player to walk five times in a postseason game and scored twice. Baltimore pitchers walked 11, their most in a game since 2019, and six of those runners scored.

Texas became the first team in postseason history with seven hits and seven walks through three innings, according to Sportradar.

Rangers designated hitter Mitch Garver rounds the bases after hitting a grand slam in Game 2 against Baltimore.

Texas catcher Jonah Heim tries to make the tag at home plate against the Orioles' Gunnar Henderson in Game 2.

Peak Performance

Seager Adds to Postseason Legacy; Rangers Set Date with Astros

ARLINGTON, Texas —

COREY SEAGER IS STILL GOING DEEP IN TEXAS during the postseason. This time he is doing it for the Rangers, who are streaking through October.

Seager and Adolis García homered early, Nathan Eovaldi pitched seven smooth innings in another playoff clincher and Texas completed an AL Division Series sweep of the Baltimore Orioles with a 7-1 victory in Game 3.

The Rangers, whose loss at Seattle on the last day of the regular season made them a wild-card team instead of the AL West champion, have since won all five of their postseason games. They are headed to the American League Championship Series for the first time since 2011.

"We had our work cut out going on the road against Tampa and Baltimore. Just shows the toughness with this ballclub and the deal with having to fly to Tampa," said Texas manager Bruce Bochy, a three-time World Series champion with San Francisco who is now going to his first ALCS. "Trust me, they wanted to win one more game in the worst way. Didn't happen ... they put it behind them."

Baltimore won an AL-high 101 games and was never swept in a series during the regular season, but the surprise AL East champions are done after a sweep at the most inopportune time. The Orioles have lost eight playoff games in a row over the past 10 seasons.

"Really proud of our group. They defied all the odds. Nobody gave us a chance," Baltimore manager Brandon Hyde said. "These guys played their butts off for six months. We just didn't play well for these last three, unfortunately."

Seager pulled a 445-foot drive into the right-field seats in the first inning, and García's three-run homer — one the All-Star slugger admired while taking a few slow steps out of the batter's box — made it 6-0 in the second to chase Orioles right-hander Dean Kremer, the Israeli-American pitcher making his first career postseason start.

"We've just been playing good ball," Seager said. "Can't say enough about what our pitching staff has been able to do."

It was the first Rangers playoff game at Globe Life Field, the stadium that was brand new in 2020 when it hosted much of MLB's neutral postseason during the COVID-19 pandemic.

The Los Angeles Dodgers spent most of that October there, and Seager was the MVP in both the NLCS and World Series.

A year later, when Texas was coming off a 102-loss season, the shortstop signed a $325 million, 10-year deal with the Rangers — and he occupies the same locker he did during that most unusual postseason with limited attendance.

Texas players celebrate on the field after sweeping the Orioles to advance to the ALCS.

With a full house for his first home playoff game with the Rangers, Seager sent the record sellout crowd of 40,861 into a frenzy when he connected in his first at-bat. He went deep seven times for the Dodgers here in 2020.

"That's what he does. He's done it before in the big moments," said Marcus Semien, the second baseman who signed with Texas for $175 million over seven years the same week as Seager's deal. "He picks his game up in the playoffs. It'll be really fun to see what he can do as we move on."

Nathaniel Lowe also homered for Texas, a solo shot in the sixth. Lowe had led off the Rangers' five-run second inning with a lineout to left, but that came on the 15th pitch of the at-bat after fouling off nine two-strike pitches.

"I saw a team that was really motivated," Bochy said. "The offense, everybody was doing something to contribute."

Eovaldi threw 76 of 98 pitches for strikes without a walk while allowing only one run and striking out seven. He was serenaded with chants of his name as he walked off the mound after the seventh — and then was prodded out of the dugout by García to tip his cap to the crowd. Eovaldi also won the Wild Card Series clincher at Tampa Bay last Wednesday.

"I've never had a curtain call or anything like that, but our fans were bringing it all night long," he said. "When I walked out at 6:30 tonight, they were chanting, the 'Let's go Rangers.' I knew it was going to be a really good night for us."

....

Rangers starter Nathan Eovaldi delivers a pitch during Game 3 of the ALDS.

Texas first baseman Nathaniel Lowe connects against Baltimore in Game 3 of the ALDS.

Marcus Semien celebrates in the locker room with teammates after winning the ALDS.

Game 1: Rangers 2, Astros 0
Oct. 15, 2023

Excited and Confident

Taveras Homers, Montgomery Shuts Down Astros in Game 1

HOUSTON —

JORDAN MONTGOMERY OUTDUELED JUSTIN VERLANDER and the Texas Rangers received a big boost from their youngest player to open the AL Championship Series with a 2-0 win over the Houston Astros.

Montgomery pitched five-hit ball over 6 1/3 innings, Leody Taveras provided a two-run lead with his solo homer in the fifth and the Rangers remained perfect in the postseason at 6-0.

Evan Carter, a rookie who just turned 21 on Aug. 29, doubled and scored in the second and made two nifty defensive plays in left field. He's shined this postseason after not making his major league debut until Sept. 8.

"He just has so much confidence," Texas manager Bruce Bochy said. "He's got the youthful enthusiasm and he's just excited to be here. He's not in awe of anything, just no fear in this kid since he's come up."

In the ALCS for the first time since back-to-back appearances in 2010-11, the Rangers swept the Rays in the Wild Card Series and the Orioles in the Division Series. The winning streak followed loses in their previous six playoff games against Toronto in the ALDS in 2015 and 2016.

"We just found a way to get a couple of runs across the board," Bochy said. "That was the difference in the game, obviously. But our guy was really good, Monty, terrific job he did. And he got in a couple of jams there and found a way to get out of it."

The defending champion Astros, in the ALCS for a seventh straight year, had a tough time getting anything going against Montgomery. The top four batters in Houston's lineup were 2 for 12 with five strikeouts against the left-hander. Slugger Yordan Alvarez struck out against him three times.

"Overall, just didn't do enough tonight, offensively," Houston third baseman Alex Bregman said. "I thought J.V. threw the ball tremendously, but we need to string together some better at-bats."

Houston's offensive woes came after it hit 16 homers and outscored the Rangers 39-10 in a three-game sweep in September. Things were much different in the first postseason meeting between these in-state rivals as they managed just five singles.

"Sometime you've got to say: 'Hey, the guy threw a great game tonight against us, excellent game,'" manager Dusty Baker said. "And they say good pitching beats good hitting, but when you don't hit, everybody wants to know what's wrong. There's not a whole bunch to say. He threw a real good game against us."

Montgomery has been great in the last month, allowing just two earned runs over 27 innings in his last four starts of regular season, and posting a 2.08 ERA in three postseason starts.

Texas starting pitcher Jordan Montgomery throws during the first inning of Game 1 against Houston.

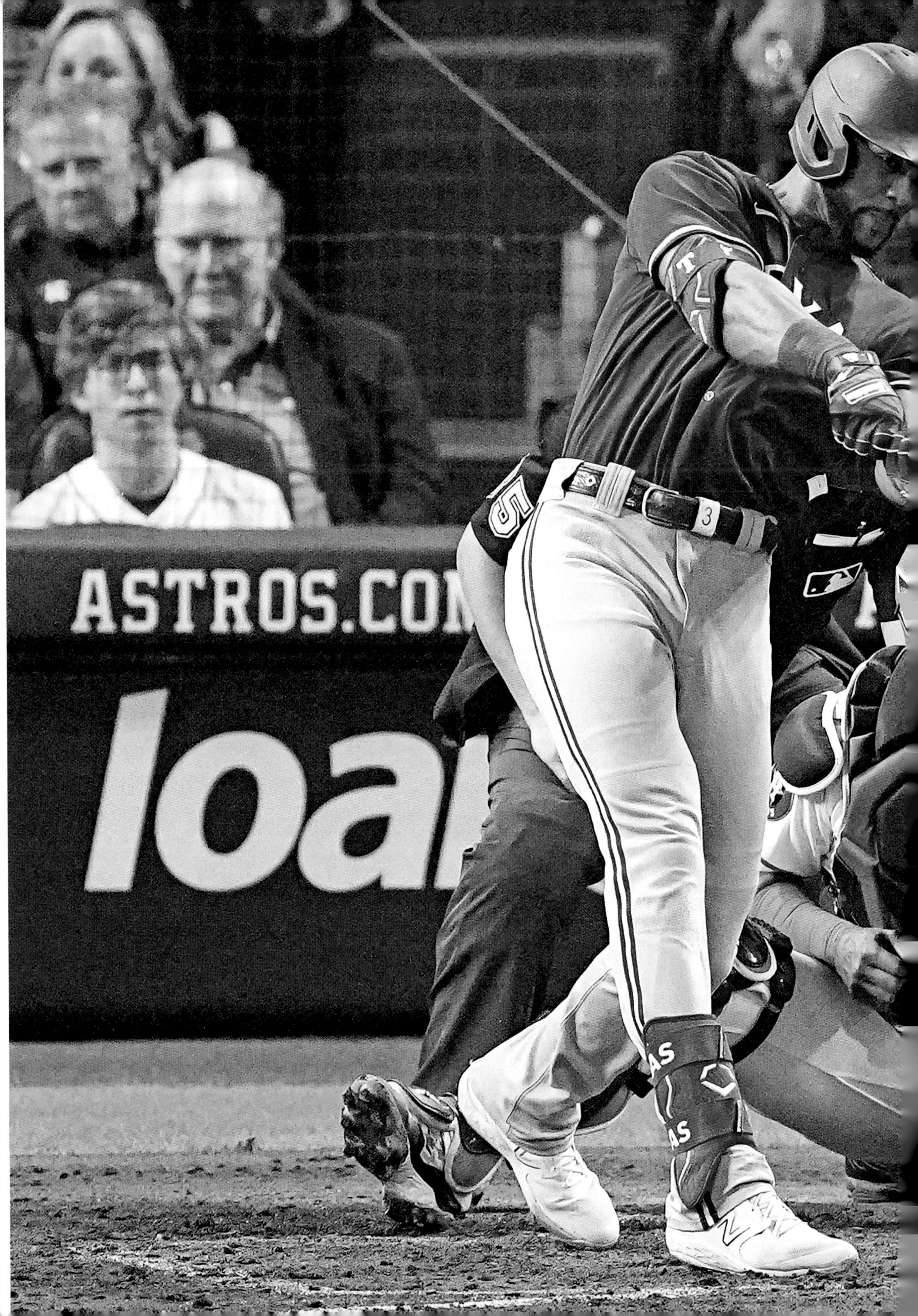

The Rangers' Leody Taveras hits a home run during the fifth inning of Game 1.

Game 2: Rangers 5, Astros 4
Oct. 16, 2023

Rising to the Moment

Rangers Build Big Early Lead, Hold On for 2-0 Series Lead

HOUSTON —

NO MATTER THE PLACE OR THE MOMENT, the Texas Rangers are rolling right now.

Jonah Heim homered, Nathan Eovaldi pitched six effective innings and Texas beat Framber Valdez and the Houston Astros 5-4 for a 2-0 lead in the AL Championship Series.

The Rangers improved to 7-0 in the playoffs, including six wins on the road. They swept the Rays in the Wild Card Series and the Orioles in the Division Series, and then posted a 2-0 win at Houston in the ALCS opener.

"It's just baseball to us," Texas third baseman Josh Jung said. "We're jumping on teams early, and that helps us settle in. Our pitching has been outstanding. You can't ask for anything more than what they've given us."

Adolis García, Mitch Garver and Nathaniel Lowe each hit an RBI single during Texas' four-run first inning against Valdez, and José Leclerc closed it out for the Rangers after Yordan Alvarez powered an Astros rally.

Eovaldi struck out nine, including two in a row after Houston loaded the bases with none out in the fifth. He was charged with three runs and five hits in his third win this postseason.

"You're talking about one of the elite pitchers in the game," Texas manager Bruce Bochy said. "They have that ability to turn up a notch when they had to. We made an error, bases loaded, and it's about picking each other up, and he picked us up there and made great pitches."

The Rangers are the fifth team in MLB history and first since the Astros last season to win their first seven postseason games. Kansas City holds the record with an eight-game win streak to start the 2014 postseason.

Alvarez hit two solo drives to become the sixth player in MLB history to have two multihomer games in one postseason. The second one was off Aroldis Chapman, trimming Houston's deficit to 5-4 with two out in the eighth. Leclerc then came in and walked José Abreu and Michael Brantley, but Chas McCormick grounded out to end the threat.

Jeremy Peña flied out to deep right field for the first out in the Houston ninth. Yainer Diaz then grounded out and Jose Altuve flied to center, giving Leclerc his second save of the series.

The Rangers jumped all over Valdez. Marcus Semien smacked the first pitch to center field for a single. Corey Seager singled to left on the second pitch before Valdez made two errors on one play.

Valdez bobbled a chopper hit by Robbie Grossman for an error that allowed him to reach first and Semien to score. His second error occurred when he badly overthrew first to move Grossman to second and Seager to third.

Valdez put his hands on his knees and shook his head at the end of the play.

Adolis García hits an RBI single during the first inning of Game 2 against the Astros.

Texas' Leody Taveras hits a triple during the sixth inning of Game 2.

A Rough Outing

Scherzer Battered as Astros Get Back Into Series

ARLINGTON, Texas —

MAX SCHERZER WAS ROUGHED UP AGAIN by the Houston Astros, this time in Game 3 of the AL Championship Series.

The Texas Rangers right-hander, who missed more than a month with a right shoulder strain, says he'll be ready for another shot at the in-state rival if needed.

Scherzer lasted four innings, leaving with a five-run deficit in an 8-5 loss to the Astros that cut the Rangers' series lead to 2-1.

"I don't know exactly how I'll be used from here on out," Scherzer said. "But my arm feels good. That's the No. 1 thing."

The three-time Cy Young Award winner gave up three runs in the second on a wild pitch and Martín Maldonado's two-run single, then allowed Jose Altuve's leadoff homer in the third. Houston took a 5-0 lead on Mauricio Dubón's RBI single in the fourth, when Scherzer struck out Jeremy Peña and Maldonado with a man on.

"I still feel like I had more in the tank," said Scherzer, who threw 63 pitches. "Given what the score was and how the game was unfolding, I get why they pulled me. I 100% agree with it."

Scherzer was dealing with forearm tightness six weeks ago when he allowed seven runs — all on three homers — over three innings in the Astros' 12-3 win. He exited after 5 1/3 scoreless innings six days later, on Sept. 12 at Toronto, before going on the injured list.

Scherzer had his second consecutive rough postseason start, allowing five runs and five hits with a walk, a hit batter and four strikeouts. In the NL Wild Card Series with the New York Mets last season, he gave up seven runs and seven hits, including four homers, over 4 2/3 innings in a 7-1 loss to San Diego.

Scherzer was acquired by Texas from a Mets in a deadline deal this summer.

As he left the field in the fourth inning, Scherzer stopped for a brief conversation with manager Bruce Bochy as he reached the dugout, with Bochy pointing toward the bullpen. Rookie left-hander Cody Bradford replaced the eight-time All-Star in the fifth.

"I was trying to communicate how I felt," Scherzer said. "I'm not second-guessing any decisions, but it's also my job as the starting pitcher to communicate how I feel. I still felt strong. I still feel like I could get outs. Then it's up to them to make the decision whether they want to use me or not."

The 39-year-old right-hander became the second pitcher to start for five teams in the postseason following appearances for Detroit, Washington, the Los Angeles Dodgers and the New York Mets. Scherzer has a 7-8 postseason record in 28 games.

....

The Astros' Jose Altuve hits a home run off Texas starting pitcher Max Scherzer during Game 3 of the ALCS.

Nightmare at Home

Astros Once Again Pound Rangers at Arlington, Even ALCS

ARLINGTON, Texas —

HOUSTON MANAGER DUSTY BAKER and third baseman Alex Bregman really have no explanation for why the Astros have been so good in that other retractable-roof stadium in Texas.

"I have no clue, to be honest with you," Bregman said. "But I think the focus has been really good in that clubhouse."

They do know the 250-mile trip north and another big-scoring road game against the Rangers has pulled Houston even in the AL Championship Series.

José Abreu hit a three-run homer right after Yordan Alvarez's go-ahead sacrifice fly, and the Astros rolled to a 10-3 victory in Game 4. They led 3-0 only four batters into the game, and responded immediately after Texas tied it on Corey Seager's opposite-field homer in the third inning.

Adolis García also homered for the wild-card Rangers, who have dropped two games in a row at home after starting this postseason with seven consecutive wins — six on the road. That included sweeps of the AL's two winningest teams, Baltimore and Tampa Bay.

"Nobody thought it was going to be easy," Texas manager Bruce Bochy said. "(The Astros) have played very well in this ballpark. We need to change that."

Game 5 is Friday afternoon at Globe Life Field, where the defending World Series champion Astros are 8-1 this season. The home team has yet to lead in this ALCS, which switches back to Houston for Game 6 on Sunday night.

"They keep asking me that same question," Baker said about his team's success in Arlington. "I've got the same answer: I don't know."

Jose Altuve had three hits in his 100th career postseason game and scored three runs for a record sixth time. Alvarez drove in three, giving him 13 RBI already this postseason, and Chas McCormick added a two-run homer.

"It makes it even more special because we won," said Altuve, the seventh big leaguer to play in 100 postseason games. "Nothing's done yet, but to be able to get the opportunity to come back and tie the series ... it's really important for us."

The Astros have outscored Texas 74-32 in winning their last seven games at Globe Life. They won 8-5 in Game 3 of the first postseason series between the instate AL West rivals.

"They crush the ball here, man. I don't have an answer other than that," Rangers first baseman Nathaniel Lowe said.

"Maybe it's too nice in the visiting clubhouse and we need to maybe switch up the spread, leave something uncooked a little bit."

Yordan Alvarez of the Astros hits an RBI single during the first inning of Game 4 of the ALCS.

Suddenly, on the Brink

Altuve Homers after Benches Clear, Houston Takes Command

ARLINGTON, Texas —

JOSE ALTUVE THRIVES UNDER PRESSURE for the Houston Astros, able to stay calm in the biggest October moments even after another bench-clearing fracas against the Texas Rangers.

The defending World Series champions are one win from a third consecutive pennant after Altuve's three-run homer in the ninth inning of a wild and testy 5-4 victory over their instate division rival gave the Astros a 3-2 lead in the AL Championship Series.

"He's got a high concentration level, because that's what it takes in big moments like that, is concentration, desire, and relaxation all encompassed into one. And everybody can't do all three of those things," Houston manager Dusty Baker said. "This dude is one of the baddest dudes I've ever seen, and I've seen some greats."

Baker wasn't in the dugout when Altuve hit his 26th career postseason homer, second in major league history behind Manny Ramirez (29). The skipper was ejected an inning earlier after the benches and bullpens cleared.

Rangers slugger Adolis García, who punctuated a go-ahead homer in the sixth with an empathic bat spike, became irate when Bryan Abreu hit him on the left arm with a 98 mph fastball. García immediately turned around and got in the face of catcher Martín Maldonado — the two also jawed nose-to-nose when García touched home plate after his grand slam in Houston on July 26.

"I just reacted to the ball that came towards me," García said. "He could have hurt me, he could have injured me. I just let him know that shouldn't happen there."

While it didn't appear any punches were thrown as the teams grabbed hold of each other near home plate, the game was delayed almost 12 minutes. García, Abreu and Baker were all ejected.

After the game, umpire crew chief James Hoye told a pool reporter Abreu was ejected for throwing with intent, and García was tossed for being the aggressor.

"The guy hits a three-run homer; the next time up he gets smoked," Texas manager Bruce Bochy said. "I'd be upset, too, if I was Doli. But like I said, it just took too long to get things back in order, that's what was frustrating me."

Rangers closer José Leclerc gave up a single to pinch-hitter Yainer Diaz to open the Houston ninth and walked pinch-hitter Jon Singleton at the bottom of the lineup. The 5-foot-6 Altuve, playing in his 101st postseason game for Houston, then pulled an 0-1 changeup over the left-field fence, just beyond the glove of a leaping Evan Carter.

"Emotions are high in the postseason. You've got two of the best teams in the world competing against each other. Everybody's trying to win. I feel like that's just him," said Alex Bregman, who also homered for the Astros. "He has a slow heartbeat. He's calm under pressure."

....

The benches clear in the eighth inning of Game 5 of the ALCS between the Rangers and Astros.

World Series Back in Sight

Eovaldi's Steady Presence, García's Grand Slam Force Game 7

HOUSTON —

ONE MORE TEXAS-SIZED MATCHUP to finally settle this Lone Star State showdown.

Nathan Eovaldi remained perfect this postseason, and Mitch Garver and Jonah Heim homered early before a ninth-inning grand slam by Adolis García helped the Texas Rangers avoid elimination with a 9-2 win over the Houston Astros in Game 6 of the AL Championship Series on Sunday night.

Road teams are unbeaten in this series going into the decisive Game 7 in Houston. Cristian Javier pitches for the Astros against three-time Cy Young Award winner Max Scherzer. Javier beat Scherzer in Game 3 at Texas.

"I'm just proud of how these guys keep bouncing back," Rangers manager Bruce Bochy said. "They're amazing. They really are. They just don't let adversity get to them."

Texas and Houston had identical regular-season records (90-72), with the AL West title going to the Astros on a head-to-head tiebreaker. Now the heated rivals are tied once again, and this time the stakes are much higher — with a World Series trip on the line.

Eovaldi, who also won Game 2, yielded five hits and two runs in 6 1/3 innings to improve to 4-0 with a 2.42 ERA in the playoffs this year. The wild-card Rangers, one of six major league teams without a World Series title, are trying to return to the Fall Classic for the first time since back-to-back trips in 2010-11.

"Of course, Nate set the tone out there. How many times has he done that?" Bochy said. "And we just had great at-bats throughout the lineup."

The defending World Series champion Astros were again felled by a subpar start from Framber Valdez and lackluster play at home. Valdez was charged with five hits and three runs while striking out six in five innings to fall to 0-3 with a 9.00 ERA this postseason.

The Rangers led by two before breaking open the game with a five-run ninth, punctuated by the slam from García — who struck out his previous four times up. The slugger was booed throughout the game after being at the center of a bench-clearing scuffle in Game 5 after being hit by a pitch from Bryan Abreu.

When García knocked a pitch from Ryne Stanek into the Crawford Boxes in left field with one out, many of those fans began streaming for the exits after yet another poor showing at home by Houston.

The Astros, who are 5-0 on the road this postseason, won three in a row in Arlington wearing their orange jerseys to move within a win of reaching their third consecutive World Series. But those orange tops didn't help them as they fell to 1-4 in Houston this postseason.

....

Rangers starting pitcher Nathan Eovaldi throws during the seventh inning of Game 6 against the Astros.

Adolis García connects on a grand slam during the ninth inning of Game 6 of the ALCS.

Sweet Shots

García Homers Twice to Send AL Pennant to Arlington

HOUSTON —

ADOLIS GARCÍA AND THESE ROAD-HAPPY RANGERS are not only tops in Texas, they're best in the American League.

García homered twice and drove in five runs as the Texas Rangers reached their first World Series in 12 years with an 11-4 blowout of the Houston Astros in Game 7 of the AL Championship Series.

Corey Seager got the Rangers started with a long homer in a three-run first inning. Nathaniel Lowe also went deep to give Texas — one of six major league teams without a World Series title — its first berth in the Fall Classic since consecutive trips in 2010 and 2011.

García homered for the fourth straight game and set a record for RBI in a postseason series with 15. He had four hits, scored three times and was the obvious choice for ALCS MVP in a series that saw the road team win every game.

"He's a bad man, isn't he?" Seager said. "To be able to come into this atmosphere and get booed every at-bat and do what he did was really special. It was really fun to watch."

After winning their Lone Star State showdown with rival Houston, the resilient Rangers open an all-wild card World Series at home Friday night against Arizona or Philadelphia, who play the decisive Game 7 of their NLCS on Tuesday night.

Bruce Bochy, who came out of retirement this season to manage the Rangers, became the first skipper to win a League Championship Series with three different teams, after leading San Diego and San Francisco to NL pennants.

He and general manager Chris Young have spearheaded a swift turnaround with Texas, making its first playoff appearance since 2016 after losing 102 games in 2021 and going 68-94 last year.

"I didn't know if I'd get back in it. And here I am. I know how blessed I am," Bochy said. "We've had our streaks. We've had our injuries. They keep getting up. To come in here and beat such a great team like Houston — and congrats on their year. But it's great to be wearing the horns in Texas."

Meanwhile, the defending World Series champion Astros were finally dethroned.

Fittingly, it came at home, where they went 40-47 this year and 0-4 in this series. They won all three games at Texas and returned to Minute Maid Park a win shy of their third straight pennant, but Houston's pitching staff got pounded for 20 runs in the final two games of the team's seventh consecutive ALCS.

"That finished our season — not being able to win at home," said outfielder Chas McCormick, who sat stone-faced in the dugout long after the last out. "That came and bit us."

The Rangers party on the field after winning Game 7 of the ALCS against the Astros, 11-4.

No club has repeated as World Series champion since the New York Yankees won three straight from 1998-2000.

"I don't like tipping my cap to anybody," Astros manager Dusty Baker said. "But when someone beats the hell out of you, what are you going to do?

"We have been spoiled around here as far as winning and winning and winning. And heck, I've been here four years, and we've been to two World Series and two Championship Series. We have nothing to be ashamed of or nothing to hold our head down about. We're down, but we're not out. And every team in baseball would trade to have had the last four years that we've had."

Texas led the AL West for most of the year, only to squander the division crown to Houston with a loss at Seattle on the final day of the regular season that sent the streaky Rangers on the road to begin the playoffs.

Turns out, that was no problem.

They have gone 8-0 away from home in these playoffs, joining the 1996 Yankees as the only teams to win their first eight road games in one postseason.

García, part of those clubs that lost nearly 200 games over the past two seasons, is savoring October success.

"More than anything, it's not even about beating the Astros or that particular opponent," he said through a translator. "It's how proud I feel about the journey we've been on and how we've been able to improve to get to this point right now where we're celebrating this victory."

....

Adolis García rounds the bases after a solo home run during the third inning.

Adolis García hits a two-run scoring single during the fourth inning of Game 7 against Houston.

Rangers manager Bruce Bochy celebrates with the trophy after winning the ALCS.

Unstoppable, Unflappable

García Lifts Rangers to World Series With MVP Showing

BASEBALL'S TOUGHEST TEAM JUST REACHED the game's ultimate destination on the shoulders of baseball's toughest guy.

The Texas Rangers proved the former, gritting their teeth when 90 wins weren't good enough to win their division, when they had to spend two weeks on the road simply to get in the playoffs and survive the first two rounds. When they had the game's stubborn dynasty on the ropes, only to let victory slip through their hands and be forced to save their season on hostile ground.

Adolis García proved the latter.

Debatable, you say? Well, perhaps he already did: Immigrating from Cuba to pursue the game at its highest level, grinding through an apprenticeship in Japan, unwanted by his first major league team – that's just a bit more than your average stateside showcase pony might endure through his 20s.

Yet when García was struck by a 98-mph fastball in Game 5 of this American League Championship Series on Friday, angrily reacted to the opponent he thought (perhaps correctly) orchestrated it all, only to become a target for zealous fans when this ALCS returned to Minute Maid Park, it was the truest test any ballplayer could face.

Games 6 and 7 in Houston would be a proving ground, for both a national audience and even teammates who greatly respected his talent but wondered how he'd react.

Striking out four times in Game 6 only heightened the intrigue.

"You never know," says veteran pitcher Max Scherzer, tasked with starting Game 7 on Monday night for a trip to the World Series. "But it always comes down to the human and how they respond.

"And he responded in a big way."

In a record-breaking, pennant-winning way.

García blasted Game 6 wide open with a grand slam and then, with everything on the line in Game 7, pummeled the Astros, his swagger and his joy and the record books bursting with every swing.

RBI single off the left field wall. Stolen base. Home run. Two-run single. Home run to right field, just for the heck of it.

And when it was over, when the 11-4 pounding of the Astros was complete and the Rangers captured the series 4-3 and punched their ticket home for the World Series, there was little doubting exactly what García exemplifies.

"He's a bad man," says Rangers shortstop Corey Seager, who jump-started the party with a solo home run in the first inning. "To come into this atmosphere and be booed every at-bat and

Adolis García holds up the ALCS MVP trophy. García started the World Series strong before an injury in Game 3.

put together the ABs he had in big moments, it was fun to watch."

Fun? Here's fun:

- Two multi-homer games and at least one homer in four consecutive games.
- Fifteen runs batted in, a playoff record – any series, any decade.
- Twenty RBI in the first 12 playoff games of his career.
- And a very shiny trophy he'll have forever as MVP of this ALCS.

More important, it showed how he exemplified what the Rangers have done.

'He's got the swag to go with it'

After playing 15 of their last 19 games on the road – a stretch that included a seven-game season-ending road trip in which they had to earn playoff qualification – the Rangers might feel in the lap of luxury back in their multi-billion dollar North Texas home.

They will open the World Series Friday at Globe Life Field, able to spectate Tuesday night when the Arizona Diamondbacks and Philadelphia Phillies play Game 7 of the NLCS, for the right to meet the Rangers.

It will be hard to lose their edge, given what they just accomplished.

"You look," manager Bruce Bochy said amid sprays of alcohol in the Rangers' clubhouse, "at what we had to do: Came in here, we won two."

Put more simply: The Rangers kicked the Astros' butts.

"We traveled here and we scored 20 runs in two games," says second baseman Marcus Semien. "That's what we needed to do to win the series."

Adolis García connects during a regular-season game against the White Sox in July.

91

Always Mr. Reliable

Seager Remains Steady in the Dugout and Dangerous at the Plate

MAX SCHERZER THOUGHT THE ANSWER was obvious. Corey Seager — the quiet, maniacal hitting savant — changing? Seriously?

"No, he's the same Corey Seager," Scherzer said with a grin. "Did you ever think he would change? No."

Scherzer then erupted in laughter. He's been Seager's teammate for two half-seasons — in 2021 with the Dodgers and this year with the Texas Rangers. In between, Seager signed one of the richest contracts in North American sports history, leaving one of baseball's marquee franchises to become the face of a resurgent team while cementing his place as one of the best hitters in the majors. All that change theoretically could change a person, even just a little bit. But not Seager.

Across the way from Scherzer, between sections 107 and 108 along the third base line at Globe Life Field, Seager's demeanor during World Series media day suggested nothing's changed. The shortstop was indifferent with reporters. His answers to questions about himself weren't expansive. He seemed almost uncomfortable with the attention. He was asked about rarely showing emotion on the field either.

"It's just kind of my personality," Seager said.

His on-field production also hasn't changed. Three years after leading the Dodgers to the 2020 title in the Texas bubble with NLCS and World Series MVP performances, Seager returned to that stage on the same field with the home team against the Arizona Diamondbacks for Game 1 of the World Series on Friday. And he continued mashing at Globe Life Field under the brightest lights.

With the Rangers facing a two-run deficit with one out in the ninth inning, Seager jumped on a first-pitch, 94-mph fastball from Diamondbacks closer Paul Sewald and launched it for a tying home run. Two innings later, Adolis García, the ALCS MVP, delivered a walk-off home run to give the Rangers a 6-5 comeback win.

Seager's blast was his 17th career postseason home run — behind only Derek Jeter and Carlos Correa for most by a shortstop in Major League Baseball history. He's hit 10 of them at Globe Life Field; just six other players have that many playoff home runs at one venue. His instant reaction to No. 10 — a roar as the ball traveled through the air — was identical to the one he mustered when he clubbed a go-ahead home run off Justin Verlander in Game 2 of the 2017 World Series. His postseason résumé dwarfs most of his contemporaries.

"Big-time players do big-time things in big-time moments," Diamondbacks manager Torey Lovullo said after his club's crushing defeat.

Earlier this month, days after the Diamondbacks swept the Dodgers in the NLDS for another shocking early playoff exit, Dodgers president of baseball operations Andrew Friedman offered

Corey Seager celebrates his game-tying home run in Game 1 of the World Series against Arizona.

a different take on Seager's ability to step up in October. When asked if teams could be specifically built for postseason success, Friedman, unsolicited, brought up Seager.

"We've had guys who've been incredible one year, not good the next, mediocre one year," Friedman said. "It's not just like, 'Oh, he is a postseason player. He is not.' It's just not that simple. And we've seen it firsthand. I mean, look at Corey Seager, 2019, 2020, 2021. I mean, there are so many examples of guys that, it's just not that easy to be like, 'Oh, let's just get the guy who's going to perform in October.' Because if it was, I promise you we would do that."

Seager went 3 for 20 (.150) with one double in five playoff games in 2019. The next year, he orchestrated the most productive postseason in Dodgers history, batting .328 with eight home runs and a 1.171 OPS in 18 games to help win the Dodgers' first World Series in 32 years. More struggles followed in his final 12 games as a Dodger in 2021. He finished that postseason 9 for 48 (.188) with two home runs and a .639 OPS.

This year, he's reverted to his 2020 postseason form. In 13 games, he's batting .327 with four home runs, five doubles, 14 walks to eight strikeouts, and a 1.157 OPS.

And for the first time, it's with the Rangers, the team that decided to build around him.

Corey Seager is greeted in the dugout after a home run against Arizona.

'The Time of My Life'

Bruce Bochy Eschews Retirement for Another World Series Run

BRUCE BOCHY WAS HOME THE PAST THREE OCTOBERS, doing a little fishing and hitting a few golf balls after stepping away from a 25-year managerial career that included three World Series championships.

As enjoyable and relaxing as that all was, he found himself missing more and more where he preferred to be this time of the year.

Bochy is back in the dugout for the postseason in his first season with the Texas Rangers, whose general manager is one of his former pitchers who lured him out of his brief retirement.

"I'm having the time of my life," said the 68-year-old Bochy, who is going to his first American League Championship Series.

The Rangers were mired in a string of six consecutive losing seasons. With Bochy in charge, they went 90-72 before sweeping the first two rounds in these playoffs against the AL's winningest teams this year — Tampa Bay in the Wild Card Series, then Baltimore in the Division Series.

"You look at a man like Boch that's done it all in this game, that's been there, done that," outfielder-designated hitter Robbie Grossman said. "From Day 1 in spring training the belief was there. He's led us the whole way."

All this was before a dramatic ALCS win over the Houston Astros.

"Hey, now me and Bruce Bochy need to battle," said 74-year-old Astros manager Dusty Baker. "I know Bruce and he knows me."

Bochy is the seventh manager to take three different franchises to a League Championship Series, and the first to win them with three different teams. He led the San Diego Padres to their last World Series in 1998, and won his three titles with the San Francisco Giants in 2010, 2012 and 2014 — the first of those wrapped up with a Game 5 win over the Rangers in their old stadium across the street from where they play now.

His 58 postseason victories are fifth on the career list, part of a .598 winning percentage in his nine trips to the playoffs. Bochy is 2,093-2,101 (.499) in regular-season games over 26 seasons, ranking 10th for wins. The only active manager with more postseason and regular-season wins is Baker, whose Astros became the AL West champion on a head-to-head tiebreaker after both teams won 90 games this season.

"He was a great manager in 2006 when I played for him, but the game has changed immensely since then," Rangers GM Chris Young said. "He managed through '19 and got to evolve then too. But to see him just step right in and be able to handle this, rules have changed since then, there's a lot that's changed in that time period. He's a great manager because he's continued to grow and evolve and be open-minded."

Bruce Bochy became the first manager to advance to the World Series with three different teams.

There were no three-batter minimums for pitchers or pitch clocks the last time Bochy managed in the playoffs, when he had a knack for matching up certain pitchers against specific hitters. But he still has plenty of opportunities to go with his hunch. Take Game 2 of the ALDS against Baltimore when Bochy inserted Mitch Garver into the third spot in the batting order — and he hit a grand slam.

The Rangers were on a 108-win pace in early June, even after two-time Cy Young Award winner Jacob deGrom had season-ending elbow surgery. They had five All-Star starters, but then all but one of them spent time on the injured list after the midsummer break. Three-time Cy Young Award winner Max Scherzer, who was acquired at the trade deadline, hasn't pitched since mid-September because of a muscle strain in his shoulder.

"It's been a little bumpy, the ups and downs, but it's been a great ride," Bochy said. "You have to savor it, enjoy these rides, appreciate them."

"No matter the ups or downs, he's going to have a cool head and keep his composure. He's got that steady nature about him. There's just never any panic."

Rangers All-Star catcher Jonah Heim on Bruce Bochy

Bruce Bochy celebrates after the Rangers clinched the AL pennant against Houston.

Two Swings, One Win

Against the Wall, Rangers Rally Past D-Backs in Series Opener

ARLINGTON, Texas —

ADOLIS GARCÍA TOOK A FEW STEPS while watching the ball before tossing his bat aside after another big swing this postseason. This one won an extended Game 1 of the World Series for the Texas Rangers.

Once his drive cleared the right-field wall in the bottom of the 11th, two innings after Corey Seager's tying two-run homer, García thrust his right arm high into the air as he started a trot around the bases that ended with him being mobbed at home plate — and a 6-5 victory over the Arizona Diamondbacks to start this surprise World Series of wild-card teams Friday night.

"He's on another planet," Rangers rookie Josh Jung said. "Every time he steps into the box it's like, grab your popcorn. ... I have no words. It's just like, wow."

Miguel Castro entered to face García with one out, and the Cuban slugger known as El Bombi drove a 3-1 sinker the other way into the second row of seats beyond a leaping Corbin Carroll. It was García's second RBI of the game, setting a record for most in one postseason with 22.

García has homered in five consecutive games, tied for the second-longest streak in postseason history, and he delivered the first walk-off homer in the World Series since Max Muncy connected leading off the 18th inning of Game 3 for the Los Angeles Dodgers in 2018 against Boston and Nathan Eovaldi — who started for the Rangers in this one.

"It was an exciting moment," García said. "I was just looking to the dugout, looking at all my (happy) teammates."

García, the AL Championship Series MVP, also had an RBI single in the first following rookie Evan Carter's run-scoring double. He finished with three hits and reached base five times.

He was hit on the left hand by a 92-mph fastball in the ninth but shook it off and promptly stole second base.

"I got lucky that it's nothing worse," García said.

In the first extra-inning game of this postseason, Texas became the first team to win a World Series game when trailing by multiple runs in the ninth since the 2015 Kansas City Royals in their clinching Game 5 against the New York Mets.

Seager tied it in the ninth when he drove closer Paul Sewald's fastball deep into the right-field stands with one out after the inning began with No. 9 hitter Leody Taveras drawing a walk.

"Everyone just started jumping for joy," García said. "We were able to exhale."

Normally pretty stoic, Seager had another emphatic show of emotion this postseason, immediately turning and yelling toward the dugout with the ball headed for the seats. He thrust both arms into the air when he rounded first base.

Adolis García hits a game-winning solo home run in the 11th inning of Game 1 of the World Series against Arizona.

"He might have turned it up a notch, to be honest. He saved us there," Rangers manager Bruce Bochy said. "You can see it in him. He gets everybody fired up."

José Leclerc retired all six batters he faced for the win, and five Texas relievers combined for 6 1/3 scoreless innings.

The blown save for Sewald, first in seven chances this postseason, was the first glaring blip for a Diamondbacks bullpen.

"It's frustrating. This is how the game goes sometimes. And we've got to find a way to be resilient and adaptable and come out with a clean mind and do our best," Arizona manager Torey Lovullo said. "I have every reason to believe we will. We've done it a lot this year."

Seager's tying shot was similar to the solo homer he hit in Game 7 of the ALCS at Houston four nights earlier, and the reaction was as well. That one put the Rangers ahead to stay in the series clincher, with the All-Star shortstop giving a massive hand slap to third base coach Tony Beasley and jumping in the dugout with his teammates.

"Very emotional times. He hit those balls so hard. If I did that, I'd be screaming, too," Texas second baseman Marcus Semien said.

Both teams got this far after having to win Games 6 and 7 of their respective League Championship Series on the road, which had never happened in both LCS matchups since those series expanded to a best-of-seven format in 1985.

"It's going to be a really good series," García said.

....

Rangers players greet Adolis García at the plate after his game-winning home run.

Diamondbacks and Rangers players stand for the national anthem before Game 1 of the World Series at Globe Life Field.

Deflating Turn of Events

Kelly Quiets Rangers in Dominant Game 2 Performance

ARLINGTON, Texas —

MERRILL KELLY CALLED HIS four-season detour to South Korea a "Lost in Translation" experience. When he made his World Series debut, it was Texas Rangers batters who were disoriented.

The 35-year-old right-hander pitched three-hit ball over seven innings, Ketel Marte extended his postseason hitting streak to a record 18 games and the Arizona Diamondbacks routed Texas 9-1 on Saturday night to even the World Series at one game apiece.

"At this point in my career, nothing is going to shock me," Kelly said. "I think going over to Korea as a 26-year-old is way scarier than pitching in the big leagues or even in the World Series."

Kelly struck out nine, walked none and allowed his only run on Mitch Garver's leadoff homer in the fifth on a sinker at the bottom of the strike zone. His 22 called strikes were the most for a Series pitcher since Stephen Strasburg in Game 6 for the 2019 Washington Nationals.

"I thought he might go nine innings today at one point," Diamondbacks manager Torey Lovullo said, contemplating what would have been the first complete game in the World Series since 2015. "But for that to happen, 89 pitches, you've got to jump him up probably another 35. I wasn't going to let him throw 120 pitches."

Gabriel Moreno hit a go-ahead homer in a two-run fourth against Jordan Montgomery, and Tommy Pham went 4 for 4 with a pair of doubles. Arizona batters broke it open late as the young Diamondbacks rebounded quickly from an agonizing defeat the night before.

Marte had a two-run single in a three-run eighth, snapping a tie for the longest postseason hitting streak with Derek Jeter, Manny Ramírez and Hank Bauer. Marte has a hit in every postseason game he's ever played.

A night after wasting a two-run, ninth-inning lead in a 6-5, 11-inning loss, the Diamondbacks outhit Texas 16-4 — the most hits for one team in a Series game in nine years.

Emmanuel Rivera also had a two-run single, and rookie Corbin Carroll had a pair of RBI singles. Lourdes Gurriel Jr. and 38-year-old Evan Longoria each singled in a run for Arizona, which got its first World Series road win after four losses dating to 2001.

Texas has won all eight of its road games this postseason, equaling a major league record.

"We'd be naive to think that we're going to run away with four in a row against a team that really fights hard like the same way we did," Rangers first baseman Nathanial Lowe said.

Kelly went to only one three-ball count.

"Just great command. He hit his spots all night, four pitches. He was on," Rangers manager Bruce Bochy said.

....

The Diamondbacks' Emmanuel Rivera scores as Texas catcher Jonah Heim reaches for the throw during Game 2.

Super Seager

Shortstop Powers Rangers to 2-1 Lead Despite Worrisome Injuries

PHOENIX —

COREY SEAGER SMASHED A HOMER THAT ROCKETED off his bat at a speed few other mortals can match. Then he made a sliding stop and started a double play in the eighth inning that might have saved the game.

The star shortstop is once again playing at a different level in October.

That's good for the Texas Rangers, who may need more of those individual heroics after a costly victory put them ahead in this World Series.

Seager clubbed a two-run homer and turned in a terrific defensive play, Max Scherzer combined with four relievers for a gem on the mound and Texas beat the Arizona Diamondbacks 3-1 to take a 2-1 lead in the Fall Classic.

"This is what you play for. This is where you want to be at this moment," said Seager, the NLCS and World Series MVP for the Los Angeles Dodgers in 2020. "Fortunately for me, having experience with this, it's always driven me. I've been fortunate enough to be part of some good teams and experience these things."

Texas overcame injuries to Scherzer and slugger Adolis García in improving to 9-0 on the road this postseason, this time in front of more than 48,000 fans at Chase Field.

The 29-year-old Seager — in the second year of a $325 million contract — once again showed he was worth every penny on the game's biggest stage.

He smoked a two-run homer into the right-field seats as part of a three-run third after Diamondbacks rookie starter Brandon Pfaadt left a first-pitch changeup high in the zone. The ball left Seager's bat at 114.5 mph, which made it the hardest-hit World Series homer in the Statcast era, dating back to 2015.

García cut down Christian Walker at the plate with a stellar throw from right field in the second, stifling some early Arizona momentum. García exited in the eighth with tightness on his left side after appearing to get hurt on a swing. He went to a hospital for an MRI to determine the severity of the injury.

Scherzer threw three scoreless innings before leaving with back tightness. Jon Gray, Josh Sborz, Aroldis Chapman and José Leclerc combined to keep Arizona's offense quiet most of the evening.

Scherzer said he was having back spasms and would know more about his availability for a potential Game 7 over the next 48 hours.

"It's tough. We're a deep group. We'll see what happens with both of those guys," Texas second baseman Marcus Semien said about the injuries. "Adolis has been the heart and soul of our team. Hopefully it's nothing too bad. But we're a deep group."

....

Marcus Semien swings the bat on an RBI single in the third inning of Game 3 of the World Series.

Corey Seager hits a two-run home run off Diamondbacks starting pitcher Brandon Pfaadt in the third inning of Game 3.

Just One Win Away

With García Out, Semien Steps Up, Sends Rangers to Brink of Series

PHOENIX —

MARCUS SEMIEN'S TWO-RUN TRIPLE AND THREE-RUN HOMER powered Texas to a 10-run lead by the third inning, Corey Seager hit another long home run and the Rangers beat the Arizona Diamondbacks 11-7 on Tuesday night to move ahead three games to one in the World Series.

Rangers batters whipped through Diamondbacks pitching like a desert storm, taking a 10-0 lead and becoming the first team in Series history with consecutive five-run innings. Seager's third two-run homer of the Series capped the second, Semien's drive punctuated the third and Jonah Heim added an eighth-inning shot.

Texas improved to a record 10-0 on the road this postseason and moved within one win of the first title in the 63-season history of a franchise that started as the expansion Washington Senators in 1961.

Forty-two of 49 previous teams to take 3-1 leads have gone on to win the World Series. The most recent club to overcome a 3-1 deficit was the Chicago Cubs against Cleveland in 2016.

Texas scored its first 10 runs with two outs, battering an Arizona staff that needed four pitchers to get its first eight outs. Miguel Castro's wild pitch brought home the first run, and an error by Gold Glove first baseman Christian Walker — the first by either team in the Series — led to five unearned runs in the third.

Seager and Semien, All-Star middle infielders signed as free agents for $500 million combined before the 2022 season, have six RBIs each in the Series. Seager, the first shortstop with three Series homers, has four homers in his last five games dating to the AL Championship Series. After leading the Los Angeles Dodgers to the 2020 title, he could join Sandy Koufax, Bob Gibson and Reggie Jackson as the only two-time World Series MVPs.

Travis Jankowski, replacing injured slugger Adolis García in right field, singled in the second and hit a two-run double in the third in his first Series at-bats.

García, the AL Championship Series MVP, spoke at the Rangers' pregame meeting.

"We're trying to go out there and win this for him," Seager said. "It really fired the guys up."

Andrew Heaney, a 32-year-old lefty with his fifth big league team, got the win by allowing four hits in five innings. Six relievers followed, with closer José Leclerc getting the final out.

Lourdes Gurriel Jr. hit a sacrifice fly in the fourth for Arizona and a three-run homer in the eighth against Chris Stratton.

Tommy Pham had a sacrifice fly in the eighth, and Gabriel Moreno delivered a two-run single in the ninth.

....

Corey Seager, right, celebrates with Marcus Semien after both scored on Seager's second-inning home run.

The Rangers' Travis Jankowski hits a two-run double as Arizona catcher Gabriel Moreno reaches for the pitch during the third inning of Game 4.

Game 5: Rangers 5, Diamondbacks 0
Nov. 1, 2023

World Champions!

Eovaldi and Garver Rise to Occasion, Lift Rangers to Pinnacle

PHOENIX —

NATHAN EOVALDI PITCHED SIX GUTSY INNINGS, Mitch Garver broke a scoreless tie with an RBI single in the seventh and the Texas Rangers are World Series champions for the first time in their 63-season franchise history after beating the Arizona Diamondbacks 5-0 in Game 5 on Wednesday night.

Marcus Semien homered late and the Rangers, held hitless for six innings by Zac Gallen, finished a record 11-0 on the road this postseason by capping the Fall Classic with three straight wins in the desert.

In his first season with Texas, manager Bruce Bochy won his fourth title 13 years to the day after his first, which came in 2010 when the Giants beat the Rangers. He also won it all with San Francisco in 2012 and 2014.

"I was sitting in a recliner there in Nashville, just enjoying myself," said the 68-year-old Bochy, who came out of retirement to take over the Rangers.

One night after Texas took a 10-run lead by the third in a Game 4 snoozer, it finished baseball's third all-wild card Series by outlasting the Diamondbacks in a white-knuckle pitchers' duel, piling on four runs in the ninth for good measure.

Gallen took a no-hitter into the seventh before giving up an opposite-field single to World Series MVP Corey Seager, whose weak grounder found a hole. Rangers rookie Evan Carter — all of 21 years old — followed with a double into the right-center gap. Garver then delivered the first run, pumping his fist as a hard-hit grounder got through the middle of the infield to score Seager and make it 1-0.

Garver was 1 for 17 at the plate in the World Series before his huge hit.

"Everything I've ever worked for is for this moment," Semien said. "Gallen was unbelievable tonight. But we came through. Once Corey got the first hit, everybody kind of woke up. Pitching was unbelievable."

The Rangers tacked on four more runs in the ninth to break open the game. Semien's two-run homer off Paul Sewald made it 5-0. The outburst was typical of the Texas offense, which scored at least three runs in an inning 13 times this postseason.

Eovaldi pitched out of trouble all night before Aroldis Chapman and Josh Sborz finished it.

"I kind of joked around: I don't know how many rabbits I have in my hat," said Eovaldi, who improved to 5-0 this postseason. "I didn't really do a great job tonight in attacking the zone. But our defense, incredible again."

Sborz struck out four in 2 1/3 innings of one-hit ball for his first save this postseason. He threw a

Rangers relief pitcher Josh Sborz and catcher Jonah Heim celebrate after winning Game 5 of the World Series.

called third strike past Ketel Marte to end it.

It's the first title for the Rangers, whose history dates back to 1961 when they were the expansion Washington Senators. They moved to Texas for the 1972 season and came agonizingly close to a World Series championship in 2011, needing just one strike on two occasions before eventually falling to the St. Louis Cardinals.

Now, after five stadiums, roughly two dozen managers and 10,033 games, the Rangers are champions.

"We go into hostile territory everywhere we went," Sborz said. "And we just stayed calm, did our job and played the way the way we played all year."

It wasn't easy. Texas led the AL West for a big chunk of the season, but coughed up the division title on the final day of the regular season to rival Houston. The Rangers also weathered injuries to key pieces, particularly ace pitcher Jacob deGrom.

That 1-0 loss in the regular-season finale at Seattle left the Rangers with the No. 5 seed in the AL playoffs and it sent them across the country to open the playoffs at Tampa Bay, part of two-week trip that took them to four cities — two on each coast. Then Texas got its revenge against Houston, winning a hard-fought series in seven games that brought them to the World Series.

"We've just got a group of winners," first baseman Nathaniel Lowe said. "When the bus driver's driving slow, we tell him, `Hey man, you know you're driving a group of

Mitch Garver celebrates after a 7th-inning RBI single against the Diamondbacks.

119

winners,' so we believed it through and through. Maybe we struggled at home, but we got it done on the road, and we've got a special group."

Finally, the Rangers had to get past the Diamondbacks, who won just 84 games during the regular season but beat the Brewers, Dodgers and Phillies in a remarkable postseason run that finally fizzled.

"I'm sorry I didn't do my job to get us there," manager Torey Lovullo said, pausing as his voice cracked with emotion. "But I will. We all will."

Gallen was one of the best pitchers in the majors this season, starting for the National League in the All-Star Game. But the 28-year-old hadn't been as sharp in the playoffs, with a 2-2 record and 5.27 ERA over five starts.

That changed on Wednesday. With some help from his defense, the bespectacled righty was at his best, mowing down the first 14 hitters he faced before walking Lowe.

Eovaldi wasn't quite as sharp, but still matched Gallen's zeros on the scoreboard despite walking five, his most in an outing since 2013.

The Diamondbacks had some juicy opportunities to score in the first five innings, but couldn't convert, going 0 for 9 with runners in scoring position.

Eovaldi made it through six, giving up four hits and striking out five on 97 pitches.

"He was a traffic cop tonight," Rangers pitching coach Mike Maddux said.

Texas starting pitcher Nathan Eovaldi throws against Arizona in Game 5.

Texas players celebrate after winning Game 5 of the World Series.